PORTS ON THE EDGE!

EXTREME
PAINTBALL

STEVEN OTFINOSKI

Cavendish
Square

New York

Published in 2014 by Cavendish Square Publishing, LLC
303 Park Avenue South, Suite 1247, New York, NY 10010

Website: cavendishsq.com

This publication represents the opinions and views of the author based on his or her personal experience, knowledge, and research. The information in this book serves as a general guide only. The author and publisher have used their best efforts in preparing this book and disclaim liability rising directly or indirectly from the use and application of this book.

CPSIA Compliance Information: Batch #WS13CSQ

All websites were available and accurate when this book was sent to press.

LIBRARY OF CONGRESS CATALOGING-IN-PUBLICATION DATA
Otfinoski, Steven.
Extreme paintball / Steven Otfinoski.
p. cm. – (Sports on the edge!)
Includes bibliographical references and index.
Summary: "Explores the sport of extreme paintball"—Provided by publisher.
ISBN 978-1-60870-226-8 (hardcover) ISBN 978-1-62712-135-4 (paperback)
ISBN 978-1-60870-864-2 (ebook)
1. Paintball (Game)—Juvenile literature. I. Title. II. Series.
GV1202.S87O74 2013
796.2—dc23
2011030602

EDITOR: Christine Florie
ART DIRECTOR: Anahid Hamparian   SERIES DESIGNER: Kristen Branch

EXPERT READER: Chris Raehl, president, National Collegiate Paintball Association,
Chippewa Falls, Wisconsin

Photo research by Marybeth Kavanagh

Cover photo by AP Photo/Chris Park
The photographs in this book are used by permission and through the courtesy of: *AP Photo*: Chris Park, back cover, 1, 2-3, 32; *The Image Works*: Rachel Epstein, 4; *Getty Images*: John Downing, 8; Peter Dazeley/The Image Bank, 21, back cover; Chris McGrath, 23; Eduardo Parra, 27; *Newscom*: ZUMA Press, 9, 11, 15, back cover; Kristin Callahan, 30; Paul Hebert/Icon SMI AMA, 35; Luke Johnson/ZUMA Press, 37; Carl Costas/Sacramento Bee/ZUMA Press, 40, back cover; *SuperStock*: Tim Oram/age fotostock, 13, back cover; Prisma, 12, 17, 20, 29, 34, back cover; *Landov*: Alex Goodlett/The Jersey Journal, 14; Martin Ruetschi/Keystone, 19; *iStockphoto*: CollinsChin, 16; *Alamy*: Jeremy Pembrey, 24

Printed in the United States of America

CONTENTS

ONE

A GAME OF STRATEGY

IMAGINE A SPORT THAT combines the fun of both tag and hide and seek but can be enjoyed by people of any age group. Imagine a sport where mental ability is just as important as physical agility. Imagine a sport that can be played in the woods, in a grassy field, or inside a multistory building. That sport you are imagining is paintball.

Paintball is one of the newest of the extreme sports. First played a little more than three decades ago, it

⟸ SOME PAINTBALL TEAMS PLAY IN WOODED AREAS.

has been, until recently, one of the fastest-growing sports in the United States, played by children, teenagers, and adults.

BEGINNINGS

On June 27, 1981, twelve men gathered in an 80-acre cross-country ski area in Henniker, New Hampshire, to play the first multiplayer paintball game. Charles Gaines, one of the twelve, had thought up the game a few years earlier in an attempt to re-create the excitement he experienced while hunting buffalo on a trip to Africa. This initial game was started over a bet among several of the players as to who would be the better player—a streetwise city guy or an outdoorsman from the country. Among the players were a writer, a farmer, and a film producer.

The paintball guns the players used to **tag** each other were **markers** whose function up to that point had been to mark and identify trees and cattle with balls of paint. The game, based on **capture the flag**, lasted three hours, with forester Ritchie White the last person left standing. White managed to avoid being tagged while capturing all the flags and never fired a single shot from his marker.

The men continued to play their game in the woods, and the next year, Bob Gurnsey, one of the original players, marketed paintball as the National Survival Game (NSG) and opened one of the first commercial paintball fields. Some authorities on the sport, such as the owners of the website PbNation, call Gurnsey the "father of paintball." In 1983 the first NSG National Championships were held, with a cash prize of $14,000 going to the winner. The first indoor paintball facility opened the following year in Buffalo, New York.

WEEKEND WARRIORS

By the late 1980s, paintball was becoming a popular weekend sport, especially for adults who spent their weekdays sitting behind a desk in an office. For them, paintball was an exciting tension reliever and good physical fun. "It was a thrill to wake up at 5 a.m. to run

PAINTBALL'S POPULARITY ROSE DURING THE 1980S. AS TIME WENT ON, GEAR AND EQUIPMENT BECAME BETTER.

around outside all day long, like when you were a kid at camp," said Russ Paparo, who, when not dodging **paintballs**, traded stocks. "I loved diving and rolling around on the ground," said data sales executive Joe Haley Jr. "How often do you get to do that?"

In 1988 the International Paintball Players Association (IPPA) was formed to promote the game and educate the public about it. The National Professional Paintball League (NPPL) was formed in 1992 by the teams playing in national tournaments to establish a common set of rules. Although called "professional," the two leagues include both amateur and professional players and today sponsor four annual tournaments in which teams compete for up to $30,000 in prize money.

GOING TO EXTREMES

According to one source, by 2005 paintball had become the third most popular alternative sport in the United States, with 10.4 million people playing the game at least once that year. Since then, the sport's popularity

A PAINTBALL TEAM COMPETES ON A CONTAINED OUTDOOR PLAYING FIELD.

has leveled off. In 2013, 6 to 7 million Americans played paintball.

Those players who wanted more action began to play an extreme version of the game called **speedball** in the mid–1990s. Speedball is played mostly outdoors in a small space that is half the size of a football field. Players stalk each other from behind inflatable barriers called **bunkers** that come in every size and shape. **Xball** is basically the same as speedball, but is played as a series of games instead of one game. One point is scored for every win, and the team with the most points at the end of thirty minutes is the winner.

The best professional speedball or **XBall** teams belonged to the National XBall League (NXL), founded in 2002. Part of the reason the league formed was to get speedball airtime on television. In the fall of 2007, the Fox Sports network aired a thirteen-episode series called *Xtreme Paintball: Beyond the Paint* that mixed lively game play with interviews with the top professional players. "XBall is the future of the sport," said the top professional player Alex Lundqvist.

PLAYERS HIDE AND DIVE BEHIND MAN—MADE BARRIERS DURING A COMPETITION.

"XBall is a really physically fit version of paintball." The NXL folded at the end of the 2008 season.

Today paintball is a sport that everyone can enjoy. Friends can get together for a fun, informal game in woods, open fields, or at an indoor facility. More serious players can compete on every level, from amateur to semipro to professional. Paintball enthusiasts can read about paintball in magazines and on Internet blogs. They can watch their favorite teams play on DVDs, the Internet, or television. Extreme paintball has truly arrived.

GETTING STARTED

PAINTBALL IS A GAME OF skill and strategy. Before you can play, you'll need two essential pieces of equipment: a paintball marker and a paintball mask or goggles. The marker fires **paintballs**, and the mask protects a player's face, especially the eyes, from paintballs. As a beginner in the sport, you may want to try renting equipment at first. Once you are hooked on paintball, you'll probably want to buy your own marker and mask.

Meet Your Marker

Markers come in all shapes and sizes, but all are essentially pistols that fire paintballs. The paintballs are stored in a **hopper**, usually located on the top of the marker. Most hoppers can hold about two hundred paintballs. When the player squeezes the trigger, a blast of compressed air or a gas (such as carbon dioxide) is released from a tank in the marker and drives a single paintball down the marker's barrel and out into the air. Players may carry the compressed gas in packs on their backs. Hoses carry the gas into the marker.

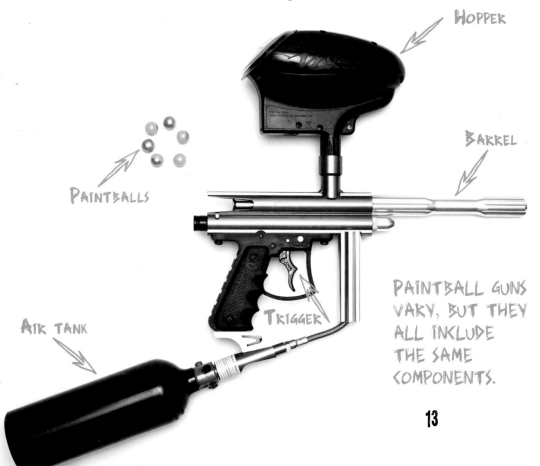

HOPPER

BARREL

PAINTBALLS

TRIGGER

AIR TANK

PAINTBALL GUNS VARY, BUT THEY ALL INKLUDE THE SAME COMPONENTS.

13

MANY PLAYERS PREFER TO USE SEMIAUTOMATIC PAINTBALL MARKERS.

A paintball can travel up to 300 feet (91 meters) per second. In most games and tournaments, to avoid injuries, there is a rule that markers cannot fire any faster than this.

The most common kind of markers are semiautomatic. A paintball drops down into the barrel with each squeeze of the trigger. However, some experts feel pump markers, which are less expensive, may be a better choice for beginners or younger paintballers. With pump markers, the balls are pumped into the barrel of the marker and fired one at a time at a lower velocity. They do not sting as much on impact.

An electronic marker has a computer chip that allows it to fire more than one shot per trigger pull. It is viewed by some paintballers as the sport's artillery of the future.

WEAR YOUR MASK

A safety mask is the most important piece of equipment for every player. Don't *ever* play paintball without one. It is designed to cover and protect your eyes, mouth, ears, and nose. Half of all paintball eye injuries result in permanent damage, with some even causing blindness. When you choose a mask, buy a good one, even if it costs more money. Inexpensive masks can fog up while you play and impair your vision.

A VITAL PIECE OF EQUIPMENT THAT ALL PLAYERS MUST HAVE IS A SAFETY MASK.

You may be tempted to take the mask off to see better, but don't—it will leave your eyes unprotected.

Balls That Go Splat

ALTHOUGH THE FIRST paintballs actually contained paint, today they do not. These tiny, round gelatin capsules or pellets contain a brightly colored, nontoxic liquid or dye. The pellets break apart on impact, and the liquid leaves a mark on a player's body or clothing. The player can later wash away the splotch left by the ball with soap and water.

THE RIGHT CLOTHING

Paintballs will not penetrate skin, but they can hurt if they hit bare, unprotected flesh. While there is no required clothing in recreational paintball, you may want to wear gloves, a long-sleeved shirt, and long pants to protect you from the sting of a flying paintball. A sweatshirt and sweatpants may offer more protection. Outdoor players wear earth-tone colors or **camouflage** to avoid being seen by opposing players in woods, fields, and other natural terrain. High-top athletic shoes or hiking boots, cross-training sneakers, and combat boots are the best footwear for playing in wooded areas.

THIS PLAYER HAS THE PROPER CLOTHES AND GEAR FOR OUTDOOR PLAY.

17

They provide strong ankle support when a player is running and dodging paintballs. Players who compete on level, grassy terrain prefer shoes with cleats.

To differentiate players on opposing teams, each team is assigned its own color. This color is featured on an armband that is worn over clothing to make it easily visible.

INDOORS AND OUTDOORS

You can play a game of paintball with friends in your backyard or in nearby woods with the owner's permission, if paintball is permitted by local laws. However, you'll probably have more fun if you go to a commercial facility to play. Such facilities are specially set up for paintball. They can be indoors or outdoors. They're also much safer, with supervised play provided by trained referees.

Outdoor facilities offer a variety of terrains to play on, from fields to forests, mountains to canyons. Indoor facilities can vary, too. They range from large, open rooms to multistory spaces with staircases and

PAINTBALL CAN BE PLAYED IN INDOOR FACILITIES THAT INKLUDE MULTIPLE FLOORS, STAIRCASES, AND ROOMS FOR PLAYING.

enclosed areas. They have objects such as bunkers that players can hide behind and fire from. Both indoor and outdoor facilities often offer such amenities as bathrooms, snack machines or food services, lockers, and rental equipment. Most important, commercial facilities provide good supervision with experienced referees to oversee play and make sure it remains safe and fair.

THE RULES OF THE GAME

PAINTBALL IS NOT ONE single game but many. The basic framework of eliminating your opponents (individuals or a team) by hitting them with paintballs shot from a marker remains the same. But the variations in the rules are numerous.

CAPTURE THE FLAG

The very first game of paintball was a form of the old game capture the flag. It remains the most popular variation of paintball today. Each team has one or more flags in its team color. The other team tries to

THE GAME CAPTURE THE FLAG IS ONE OF THE MOST POPULAR IN PAINTBALL.

capture their opponent's flag or flags and bring them back to their **flag station**. The first team to get all the flags wins. In tournament play, points are scored for each flag captured and each opponent team member eliminated. The team with the highest score at the end of the designated time period (fifteen minutes or longer) is declared the winner of that game. The number of players on each team is determined by the size of the playing field. If the field is small, there may be as few as three players. If the field is large, there may be hundreds of players on each team.

CREATE YOUR OWN STORY LINE

A more creative and challenging form of paintball is the **scenario game**. Here the players follow a particular story line, either from instructional material or one they make up themselves. The story can re-create a historical event, such as a famous battle. Players may dress up in historical costumes and portray specific historical characters. The scenario can also be fictional. Players may be fighting for survival on an alien planet

A SCENARIO PAINTBALL GAME RE-ENACTS ALLIED FORCES TAKING NORMANDY DURING WORLD WAR II.

or battling zombies in a graveyard. The possibilities are endless. Unlike capture the flag, in scenario paintball, a player who is hit or tagged can return to the playing field after a certain period of time. The game can go on for hours or even days.

Bang! Bang! You're Out!

IT'S A THRILL when you tag another player with your marker, but it's not so thrilling when you are the one who is tagged. The victim is required by the rules to hold up his or her marker and cry out "Hit!" or "Out!" Then the person must leave the playing field. If a player is hit but the paintball doesn't break open and mark him or her, the player can continue to play. Sometimes a player will cheat by wiping; that is, wiping off the splotch of paint and acting as if he or she weren't hit. If caught doing this by a referee, the player will be thrown out of the game.

Speedball and RaceTo

Speedball is an extreme sport form of capture the flag. The game is played quickly and furiously on a small playing field. Speedball is a tournament game usually played by amateurs and a few professional players that is watched avidly live and on television by its fans.

RaceTo is an extreme version of paintball that largely replaced another version, XBall, by 2009. RaceTo is played in one period, and teams switch sides every odd point. One flag is planted in the middle of the small playing field, and each team fights to get to it and bring it back to their side. When a capture is successful, players take a two-minute break before resuming play. The team with the most flag captures and "kills" wins.

Winning Strategies

Paintball, whatever variation you play, is a game of strategy. During recreational play in the woods, one team tries to invade the enemy's territory to wipe them out or capture a flag or some other item. Here are

SAFETY FIRST

PAINTBALL IS A relatively safe sport, but it can quickly become unsafe if you don't follow some basic safety rules. In the previous chapter, we mentioned the importance of wearing a safety mask or goggles. Here are four more safety rules to follow.

KEEP A BARREL-BLOCKING DEVICE IN PLACE: A marker can go off accidentally. If it hits another player after he or she has taken off a safety mask, the results can be disastrous. You *must* install a barrel-blocking device such a barrel sock on your marker to prevent this from happening.

KEEP EQUIPMENT CLEAN AND WORKING: Clean the barrel of your marker regularly, and check it for any defects. If it is not working properly, have it repaired immediately by a qualified repair person. Check goggles for cracks, and make sure to wipe them clean of dust and fog after using.

KEEP ALERT: When playing outdoors, watch out for any hazards or obstructions on the playing field, such as broken glass, litter, or sharp rocks.

KEEP TO THE RULES: Don't break the rules of the game, and listen when the referee speaks to you. His or her job is to keep the game fair and safe for everyone who is playing.

A PAINTBALL TEAM MAKES A FULL FRONTAL ASSAULT ON THE ENEMY.

some basic strategies that have helped players achieve these goals.

- **Skirmish Line**—In this defensive strategy, team members spread out and move forward toward enemy territory, hiding behind barriers and bunkers when necessary. This strategy makes it difficult for the opposing team to break through the line and invade a team's territory.
- **Full Frontal Assault**—In this offensive strategy, a team rushes their enemy in a surprise attack. While some players may be tagged, enough may penetrate

27

the opposing team and rout them while reaching the goal.

• **The Dead Man's Walk**—This clever strategy is a risky one, but it can pay off big if successful. A player begins to walk off the playing field, looking discouraged. Opposing players think he or she has been eliminated and relax their guard. Then the player, who has been playacting, turns and fires on them.

FOUR

PAINTBALL PROS

PROFESSIONAL PAINTBALL PLAYERS love what they do. They live for the thrill of the game and thrive on the excitement of being both the hunter and the hunted. Compared to other professional athletes, though, they don't pull down big salaries. Mike Paxson, a leading player for Team Ironmen, has a reported income of less than $30,000 a year. As the sport grows in popularity and television and Internet coverage increases, the money to be made on the professional circuit is increasing. In the meantime, top players vie for product endorsements and sponsorships. Other players make ends meet by pursuing second careers.

Super Player, Supermodel

Alex Lundqvist (1972–   ) has been a superstar in two highly competitive fields—professional paintball and modeling. Growing up in his native Sweden, he discovered paintball by watching the movie *Gotcha!* (1985) and became hooked. He began playing paintball in his backyard with his brother Max and their friends. Two years later, they formed their own team and eventually beat Sweden's top professional paintball team, Joy Division. Before long, Alex and Max were recruited for Joy Division.

ALEX LUNQVIST WAS SWEDEN'S TOP PAINTBALL PLAYER. HE HAS PLAYED IN THE UNITED STATES FOR TEAM GROUND ZERO AS WELL.

Alex eventually moved to the United States, where his girlfriend encouraged him to try fashion modeling.

He quickly became a top model but then returned to his first love, paintball. He was soon playing for the professional team Ground Zero and played for the World Cup team in 2000. Max moved to the United States and joined Alex on Ground Zero through 2003. "Paintball is amazing, I couldn't live without it," Lundqvist has said, "and it is an exciting time for the sport."

BEA YOUNGS PAXSON

Once the domain of men, paintball soon had a number of amateur women's teams, including the Valkyries, Fallen Angels, and Guns for Hire. The pioneering female team was the Femmes Fatales, formed in 2000. One of its first star players was Bea Youngs Paxson (1980–   ). A smart businesswoman and powerful advocate for the sport, as well as a skillful player, Youngs played with Team Destiny of Southern California, which she owns. She is also a commentator at paintball events, was editor-in-chief of *Paintball Sports Magazine*, and has taught the sport to children at paintball camps. Youngs is married

Team Dynasty – Paintball's Top Team

NO PAINTBALL TEAM has achieved the level of fame and success attained by Team Dynasty of San Diego, California. Formed in 2001, the team has won Paintball Sports Promotion's World Cup three times. In 2005 it won eight out of ten national tournament events. Among Dynasty's top players are Alex Fraige, the only original team member still on the roster in 2013, and Oliver Lang, who returned to the team in 2011 after playing for the Los Angeles Ironmen. Today, when not winning tournaments in the United States, Team Dynasty is traveling, teaching paintball, and promoting the sport around the globe.

to professional player and coach Mike Paxson. Since the birth of their daughter in 2009, she has retired from the sport to be a stay-at-home mom.

OLIVER LANG—PAINTBALL SUPERSTAR

Among the most prominent professional paintball players today is Oliver (Ollie) Lang (1983–   ). Lang started playing paintball at age fourteen and joined the Ironmen at seventeen. In 2001 he helped form the Dynasty team. Four years later, he rejoined Ironmen, becoming the first player to be offered a top annual salary of $100,000. In 2005, at age twenty-two, Lang was named the International Paintball Player of the Year. A quiet, reserved person off the field, Lang is a dynamo on the field and one of the most exciting players in the sport. According to rival player Matt Marshall, Lang "wins so frequently, plays our sport so instinctually, and gobbles up life on the road at such a frantic and furious pace, he's either possessed by demons or blessed by the gods."

A WORLD OF TOURNAMENTS

TOURNAMENT COMPETITION EXISTS on every level of play in paintball—from professional and semiprofessional to college and amateur. Today's tournaments are mostly played on open, level fields with inflatable bunkers that are staked into the ground to offer protection and hiding places for players. Organizers felt that naturally wooded areas with their varying terrain could give one team an unfair advantage over the other.

PROFESSIONAL TOURNAMENTS

Paintball Sports Promotion (PSP) absorbed the National XBall League (NXL) and its eight professional teams in 2008. PSP's professional events are aired on the Internet. The National Professional Paintball League (NPPL),

A PAINTBALL TEAM COMPETES IN THE NPPL'S SURF CITY OPEN IN HUNTINGTON BEACH, CALIFORNIA.

formed in 1992, sponsors four annual tournaments for its seven-player teams.

THE WORLD CUP

The Paintball World Cup saw its twenty-first year in October 2012 and was held at Fantasy of Flight, an aviation-themed recreational park and museum in Lakeland, Florida. A total of more than 300 teams from all over the world participated in the 2012 World Cup, which was won in the professional division by the Houston Heat. While many teams enter this tournament in hopes of winning the coveted World Cup, other teams are simply there to place high enough to raise their overall season standings.

COLLEGE AND AMATEUR COMPETITION

The National Collegiate Paintball Association (NCPA) sponsors sixty events each year. The first college paintball club was formed in 1986 at the United States Military Academy at West Point, New York.

A TEAM FROM RUSSIA COMPETES IN THE WORLD CUP AT FANTASY OF FLIGHT IN FLORIDA.

PAINTBALL AND THE X GAMES

AS OF 2013, extreme paintball, as played by many professional teams, is not part of the X Games sponsored by the Entertainment and Sports Programming Network (ESPN). One reason is that some people feel paintball, as played by amateurs around the world, does not demand the same discipline, skill, and dedication as other extreme sports. However, the rise of professional paintball is changing this perception. Many extreme paintball fans are petitioning the X Games to include their sport, and the day may not be far off when this becomes a reality.

The first intercollegiate tournament took place at Sherwood Forest in LaPorte, Indiana, in May 1994. High school finals were included in the 2011 NCPA Championships for the first time. A total of seventy-eight college and high school teams competed in three divisions, with the University of Tennessee Volunteers winning the Class A division. The championships were broadcast by Fox College Sports for the seventh consecutive year.

The level of amateur competition has risen impressively in recent years. The International Amateur Open (IAO) was begun in 1991 and was played annually in August at Three Rivers Paintball in Pittsburgh, Pennsylvania, until 2007. More than one thousand players competed in the five-day event, which was open only to amateurs.

How can you join a paintball tournament? All you need is to form a team with a group of friends and apply to join an amateur tournament in your area. You may apply in the category of skill level or age group.

Paintball is a game of strategy and skill that can be fun and challenging on every level of play. "For some,

COLLEGE LEVEL AND AMATEUR PAINTBALL ASSOCIATIONS HELP PROMOTE THE GROWTH OF THE SPORT.

being a weekend warrior is enough," writes Steve Davidson, editor of 68Caliber, a daily news website for the paintball industry. "Others play for the thrill of victory and seek out higher levels of competition. Paintball serves up plenty of opportunities for everyone. How far you go in this sport is largely up to you." So load up your marker with paintballs, get out on the field, and play ball. Paintball, that is!

GLOSSARY

bunkers barriers, often inflatable, that are used to hide behind and shoot from in a paintball game

camouflage clothing made of fabric with a design that blends into the background

capture the flag a popular paintball game in which one team tries to capture the flag or flags of an opposing team

flag station a team's base camp, where it keeps captured flags in a game of capture the flag

hopper the container on a paintball marker that holds the paintballs

marker a paintball gun

paintballs capsules made of gelatin that contain a colored dye

scenario game a paintball game that follows a story line

speedball the same game as speedball but played as a series of games within a thirty minute time limit

tag to hit with a paintball

wiping a form of cheating in which a player who has been tagged wipes off the paint mark and continues to play

XBall an extreme form of paintball based on the game center flag, in which a flag is planted in the middle of a field, and each team attempts to bring it back to its side

FIND OUT MORE

BOOKS

Dell, Pamela. *Paintball for Fun!* Minneapolis, MN: Compass Point Books, 2009.

Love, Paul. *The Paintball Question and Answer Book.* Seattle, WA: CreateSpace, 2011.

Mattern, Joanne. *Paintball.* Vero Beach, FL: Rourke Publishing, 2010.

Wendorff, Anne. *Paintball.* New York: Children's Press, 2008.

DVDs

Basic Painting: An Introduction to Scenario Paintball at the West Point Combat Classic. Scenario Paintball Films, 2009.

One with the Gun: Tournament Paintball Techniques. Bayview Entertainment/Widowmaker, 2010.

Paintball the Movie: Court Jesters. Phoenix Entertainment Group, 2009.

Tactical Paintball. Westlake Entertainment, 2007.

PaintBall.com—"Everything Paintball"

www.paintball.com

> This site has information on paintball news, events, and safety, as well as a photo gallery and ads for Internet retailers selling supplies and gear.

Paintball Times

www.paintballtimes.com

> In existence since 1993, this site includes articles on strategy, paintball history, paintball fields, and technical topics, as well as opinions, advice, discussion forums, and equipment reviews.

PbNation

www.pbnation.com

> This website includes a forum for new players and the largest directory of places to play paintball.

INDEX

Page numbers in **boldface** are illustrations.

ABOUT THE AUTHOR

STEVEN OTFINOSKI has published 150 books for young readers. His many books include more than two dozen biographies and books about animals, history, and states. He lives in Connecticut with his wife, Beverly, an English teacher and editor, and their two children.